It's Not About You, It's Not Not About You

Molly Fonseca

DEDICATION

I dedicate this to myself. In a recent poem I wrote, "that's the thing about poems, they're never about me." And to remedy that, I'll dedicate this book to myself because I deserve it and these words really aren't meant for anyone elses' eyes anyway. And if you're eyes are reading this and you're not me, you must be pretty trusted and must be new to my life because I don't think I would show this to anyone in my world currently. To me - I wouldn't be here without you, literally and figuratively.

ACKNOWLEDGEMENT

I, Molly Fonseca, acknowledge that I wrote these words and felt these things. I acknowledge that I've been feeling overwhelmed and depressed, thought about dying a lot, thought about quitting my job and never coming back to Texas occasionally. Felt stuck here because of the sunshine. I acknowledge myself.

PREFACE

I hope that if I find myself in a place to flip through this, it seems dramatic or precious, embarrassing maybe? Too vulnerable and wanting too much. Or maybe a warning to not let myself get to this place again? Just a reminder of how bad things can get when I start wanting more than this life can give. Like reading my teenage journals, it's from a different, a person who worried about too many fleeting things.

the slow fade of love

it slips. it slowly fades. and i wonder if the
gentleness of its awayness is the hardest part, the
elegance of it, the reach and stretch further and
further from my palms, my tips. it doesn't mean
to hurt, it just needs to move on, to see the other
side, a side my eyes are not quite ready for, i still
squint in the light too sharp for my senses that
have dug deeper and deeper into the darkness
lately. and sure, the pinks are stunning, the way
the oranges juxtapose them, the swirls of purples
leading into the gray of twilight and then
darkness. I know it's pretty, but sometimes don't
we all wish the sun would stay a little longer?
and i know there's laughter at this thought,
(always laughter and i try not to take it
personally. but i've grown tired of being laughed
at)
but the moon.
don't forget the moon.

against hope

hope is a fools trap. i don't need it. i'm no fool, i promised to stop being your fool, so no longer hope's fool neither. i don't understand what it's for? to keep me grounded to this ever changing groundlessness that only fools could hope to be grounded to, holding, gripping, knuckling to the no thing, the nothing that is a future? i used to get used to hanging out with hope, we had some late nights hope and i, grips leaving little moons on the inside of my palms, the indents taking years to undent. and yet here we are, wondering what it was all for. and still my inner nature, my inner-ness that has been nurtured, spoonfed to believe that hoping and wishing and faithing will bring good things to those who wait. the unforeseen forces working, promising that good things are coming if you just keep hoping , if you just keep shitting rainbows, if you just keep fucking unicorns. well, i'm tired of it. and my body is sore from the crunched over prayers, my heart, my poor heart. that muscle held out the longest, but even my heart has grown calluses against hope. whatever tomorrow brings, what more disappointment what more loss what more

lonely nights writing these words, i'll only hope
for it be like this moment here.
because this moment here is all there is and all i
could ever hope for there to be.

8 ounce champ

i googled the approximation of the weight of my heart, 8 ounces, others 10. Not much information on if that number is influenced by breakage or not, full or not, not sure if that makes a difference. And my heart, a solid 8 ounces, that's no joke by the way, although lighter I'm sure it could fight in the middle class, has stared down a few heavy hitters in its time, but these 8 ounces - are they impacted by the antidepressants i've been taking lately? pristique, just to add a bit of mystique to what my eyes open to in the late morning light, and if my heart is the most depressed, does that affect the ounces? if all the blood's been drained from face, and my anxiety causes my pulse to rise, yeah not a lot of info on that. 8 ounces is small for the beating its been taking lately, sure the ba bump if its tell tale is strong and loud, i worry that it's just working on routine, muscle memory, keeping me going just because its machinery forces it to work in that way, which i'm sure is true, i have no control over it anyway.
8 ounces.

such a small thing to be controlled by. such a
small thing to have no control over.

5

11:11

I want to believe that the cards that slip out of the deck while shuffling are special, jumping out for a purpose, no accident type of thing. I want to believe the cards themselves mean something, to trust there's some plan or path already set out for me if I'd just follow the signs, listen with more than my ears, breathe deeper and connect. To feel something when I touch the crystals, at 11:11, shooting stars, I'd even take believing in the Bible at this point. The lines on hands guide me nowhere, the lines on my face however at least show me what has been, smiles left lines, sun left damage, time left the rest. Truth is I never really believed in this stuff. I know the future isn't prefixed on a fixed point for me. I wanted to believe there was a force, some energy leading me to a higher purpose, a great service to humankind, the kind of kindness my heart used to delight at giving. I wanted so many things. And now.

The incense smells good. And the full moon is pretty. Meditation makes me sleepy. Horoscopes feel silly. But there's a ring that meant something. And songs I won't listen to. Places I'm trying to make new memories in. People who never quite clicked. I still want to believe in the path, but I fear I'm too wise to trust it will lead anywhere I actually want to go.

hold me close

i know, i know this shit gets dark. i know. i know i'm heavy lately, the smudges under my eyes, the flakes of mascara i didn't have the energy to wash off, the grease in my hair. yes, i see it too. i'm trying to focus on one day at a time, feeling my jagged feels, put the food in the mouth, get that movement rush, meet with the therapist for the therapeutical exploration of why what how, sleep, yes give it a rest, reach for that medicine that stops my brain but makes my body take a walk around the block away from me, it comes back eventually usually with a migraine companion to remind me that getting better doesn't include much feeling better. and you ask what you can do and you ask what you can do and you ask. and i answer just hold me close.

an interlude

she sneaks into my heart in the sneakiest of
ways, not like a snake and certainly not subtle,
but like a bull crashing through my aortic
chambers. she knows she needs to do it this way
which is how i know she is my true love, she
knows the ways i need to be touched, how i need
to be reminded again and again and again that
we belong together and the only way out is side
by side. she doesn't bristle at my need for
reassurance, we've been dancing this dance for
far too long now, she just kicks down the door,
crashes through the boards i boarded up around
my creativity and my passion and my drive, she
doesn't clean up after her mess. she says those
scraps will be good for kindling, now let's build
a fire.

the spark nudges my sweet tired heart from her rest.

i try to find the spark. i focus on my little writing prompts and clever wordplay, write a description of the sun that is so dark it matches the way i've been feeling lately, it's just gonna burn out like me i've burnt out. i sit outside alone with my thoughts, waiting for a phrase to catch my nose, something i follow the scent of the trail, it leads nowhere tonight. my little miseries quiet, my little heart, resting lightly. it's hard to tell if i'm just sleepy or if i've grown tired of exploring what has been exhausting me lately. but that makes me laugh, i know my little voices will return, nothing has changed so why would they have gone away, just a stroke of luck they are quelled tonight. but you asked. and i answered. and i'm writing.

there must be something i lost

i've been obsessed with my childhood, searching
for clues, scraps, some long-forgotten code,
some detail in my pre-pubescent scribblings,
keeping my eyes open way past their close time
asking why i am like this? how did i get made to
become this? my spine used to be shaped like an
s, if i'd been born in another time my uneven
shoulders would have kept turning into
themselves until my back resembled rolling hills
on the countryside, to put it nicely, like a
hunchback to put it the way the doctors put it to
me when i was 12. they cut out a chunk of my
right hip bone to fuse metal rods to my spine but
the couldn't make it straight, they left the bottom
of the s curvy and i wore a brace until i was 16
to correct that, the doctors said they wanted to
be kind to my body, because after all, i was
going to be 40 someday. i wonder if the doctors
remember these offhand remarks as i much as i
do? when they looked at the full-length x-rays
they circled my uterus and said i wasn't

developing inside as fast as i was outside. truer
words, right? and now, the jagged scar from the
nape of my neck to the small of my back
resembles a timeline more than anything else,
and i wonder if this is where it started, a flat,
shiny spot in between the tops of my shoulder
blades, if that's the beginning, where am i now?
the bottom of my shoulder blades? further
down? is this the line i need to follow to know
where i'm headed? am i reading into it? is it not
the sign, just a dotted line that gives me lower
back pain and keeps my flexibility in check? if
that's not the clue from my childhood what is? i
wore a brace until i was 16, but it was shaped
more like a corset. i was scared to take it off, i
didn't know what my body would do without its
definitions. i wore a brace until i was 16, that
has to have done some damage here somewhere,
makes me feel like i have to be strapped in to
feel safe, that being free is dangerous? i wore a
brace until i was 16 and that has to mean
something? people don't just do that and come
out normally? my parents held onto it until i was
25, it was always in the closet. i wore a brace
until i was 16 and I've always hated my body. it
started failing me way before my brain, which
started failing me the summer before i turned 21.
and while i try to say that wasn't during my
childhood, i do think 20-year-olds are kind of

like children, so maybe that's part of the story?
my brain turned into itself and it got bored with
my little dreams about acting, and making art,
and moving to anywhere somewhere that wasn't
the midwest, my brain kept turning into itself
until it resembled a brain with a bunch of lesions
on it, i'm sorry there's no other way to put it.
and all summer i had hours to think inside every
magnetic tube i was shoved in. i realized what
death meant, i learned what failing meant, i
learned i wasn't invincible. i learned not to trust
myself. i learned to trust no one but myself. it
has to mean something. i have to mean
something. and if it doesn't, if it doesn't then
what? then what? just for nothing? just for the
pain of it? to teach my young body and brain
that we start dying the moment we're born? Yes,
I know that. But why am I this way? Yes, I know
I'm going to die, for that is certain and I know
that I am dying just as fast as these letters reach
the page, reach your eyes your ears humble
reader, but the time running out doesn't tell me
what to do with the time, the grains of sand still
remaining, time running out doesn't mean I can't
look back at the collected, sift through the
haystacks searching for meaning in the dead
grass, time is running out and i have to make
some meaning of what's left of it. i have to know
why i'm here and maybe there's a bit of

understanding, some nugget to digest about how
i got here. time is running out. there must be
something i've lost.

bird brain

Do you think birds pretend they are planes flying overhead when they hear that deafening rumble? Spread their wings and dive down, startling their mom, antagonizing their little brother? To think a bird dreaming of being a machine, controlled by an operator with set flight paths. To think a bird whose wings can stretch and fly and swoop and glide would pretend to be a part of Spirit Airlines' fleet, disgruntled sardines lulling themselves to drunk inside headed to Miami for a 3-hour layover they won't catch. A bird can layover in Miami anytime, enjoy cocktails with a local cockatiel, stay for a while, think about building a nest in the nice part of town and decide nah, I'm a bird, the fuck do I want with Miami? Give me the sky, give me the wind, give me a little seed to sustain me on my flight. Give me my family, my murder, my murmur ration, my gaggle, my flock. Leave those constraints of our man-made machinery behind, little bird, you are free.

i used to think being small was ok, but i don't want it anymore.

if you take me to the middle of nowhere, i'm sure the plants will bring me peace. i'll delight on the birds, the clouds, the quiet, the stillness. the sadness of the vast aloneness would get to me. who to make art for in the wild? who to reach out to, what hand to extend to my next dance partner? i don't know how to dance to bird chirps, i'm sure i could figure it out, but i like loud music. and if you make me buy a house, i know i'd like to paint the walls big bright colors. i know i'd plant a garden. but i don't understand escrow and i don't care to either. and a mortgage weighing me down when i don't know how to swim with my student loans shackled to my toes. so, let's keep renting, there's freedom in impermanence. and while we're talking about forever, it might have been a mistake to wear a ring, i never took your name

but i we i made a promise i don't care to follow
through on. and if my brain can't make
serotonin, i guess i'll keep swallowing these
pills. i'm no longer water-sogged with tears, but
i still cry with the sun's set. and if i can't be with
the sun, i guess i'll take its moon. i remember, i
remember the sun's rays touching me all over,
the damage left all over my skin. i never got
quite used to the sun's light on me anyway,
always knew it would end like this. so, yes, i'll
take the moon, but write about the sun forever.

sheep in a yellow peacoat

several months ago, which feels like an eternity now a different lifetime perhaps, i certainly didn't predict this future here, couldn't open my eyes to this reality but at the time i was writing about being a clown, a fool in your eyes. afraid you'd laugh at me, at my silliness for your returned stare. afraid you'd see me through my tricks, my attempts send a poker my way to keep up the jig, my jiggles for your giggles. since then i've moved on to other repetitive images that feel more like me, mainly about this darkness, this weight, a desire to be free. you've read the poems. even if you hadn't. you'd know. i love you, but i can't be your fool. i burned my little costume, so what to wear now? and the bells, the bells gave me headaches but signaled to you i was around. and last night. last night. last night i remembered why the phrase fool around doesn't quite sit right. and maybe the bells would have had a different use, a warning bell to my heart, my body. maybe you never saw me as your fool,

but more a sheep in a yellow peacoat and you a
wolf in faded gym clothes.

19

it is time to fall forward

and so it is time to fall forward. is it better to land on my face or break my wrists trying to catch myself? honestly, i'll probably go the wrist route, even though i've fallen before i always protect the 8x10. i never fully let myself experience the risk of landing on my face, in October or any other month. Falling forward is my least favorite, sure you get some shut eye but the darkness and the cold. People get obsessed with sweaters scarves costumes pumpkins but the moon just reminds me how hard I fell on my wrists when i tried to catch the sun. give me the fall back where the sun and i spend more time together give me the fall back when i never sleep anyway. give me the fall back where I can't see the plunge, the landing, the drop, a weightless moment where i can make believe the splat won't leave a mark. give me the last fall back before i messed this up.

and yet, they say to not live in the past because we are not defined by it. but the last fall did a doozy on me. the last fall left me with more than bruises. and sure, i can consciously create my future, but it is defined by my injuries, the limitations from the last fall. my future comes with a heart that was broken, i taped up what i could but those muscles take time to heal. and i wince and I brace myself for this next fall forward, but i know i'll turn into it at the first chance i get, soften my landing. i create my future now but it's smaller, less risky. maybe i was never meant to land on my face, some of us aren't. i'm soft and fragile. i don't like the darkness. or the cold. the gray of the winter. i used to think i was a light, but now i just blend in.

so simple

how simple, how easy get married have children stay together for the children work through it because of the children find purpose because of the children make friends from the parents focus on them, not you. this is what we're here for, right? this is what my body was made for this is what marriage is for i don't need my own purpose i don't question the point of this ring i just need you to co-life with we don't need to make it so complicated. unified front. and put the kids first and it seems like it would be easier. not this rudderless attempting not this selfish path. it's about me. it's about my unhappiness. it's about my loneliness and what it all adds to my life just me. this little solo so low person. me and my way what can grow from here. well, not there, nothing can grow from there. i've suspected my whole life that nothing could grow from there, not a fertile soil location. but if would if could if this have been avoided?

i used to sing in the shower too.

I remember once a friend asked me the last time I cried and I told her I couldn't remember. She couldn't believe that. It's not that I ever had problems with crying but I had honestly been in a place where I hadn't felt many things that made me feel like crying. I was loving and loved. I was living a life that felt supported in a world that didn't feel kind but it didn't feel out to get me personally. The news was different then too and I wasn't on the case for a new me, a new way of being. I just was. Just being every day. And now. I can't remember the last day I didn't cry, maybe in June or July. Definitely not in August, September, or October. November and December aren't looking good either with the darkness and cold and loneliness the holidays inevitably deliver. I remember I once sang in the car, something different than Bright Eyes. And now the symbolizing in dropping my AirPods and one flying out, the other skittering away and chasing down my sunglasses flopping off from bending down to get my distraction devices seems too painful to spend much time thinking about. I hope they don't break. I'm not sure how much I can take.

this ones really not about you.

wish you would let go again. wish you would be
brave. wish you would laugh in that loud way
where the teeth in the back of your mouth show,
no one would notice the dark stains from coffee
or collection of dinner morsels. wish you could.
wish you could jump in full force, stop this toe
in tiptoe, feel those heels on the ground, both at
the same time, bend the knees and release. miss
that weightless feeling. wish you weren't so
scared, not so scared, just timid. know you hate
being called shy, but wish you weren't. wish
your heart would open again, feel connected to
the rest of you. wish you could like your
reflection again, you're really not all bad. the
way you love your pet guinea pigs and patiently
pet their fat tummies, love that you're not a dog
or cat person anymore. you want relationships
that take a little work, some patience, don't have
obvious payouts like man's best friend. the grey
in your hair is really quite stunning and the
pandemic yoga has made your shoulders quite
lovely. miss your ability to eat to a tummy ache,

know it's not the best, but is a release in its own
way, a dive into delight. you can come back with
new parts to love, won't mind that, more to love
doesn't sound bad. think we need more of that in
the world. you'll be back. just keep waiting.
made a little trail for you to catch, a collection of
mountain laurel smells, know your nose could
find in the heaviest of rose-filled rooms, left a
collection of bright yellow cloth, different
shades and patterns offset with clashing colors,
you'll find something to wear with them, made a
collection of ice creamed sweets, chocolate and
cinnamon, vanilla too, you always love the plain
option. better hurry, it could melt, but there's
leftovers in the freezer, we'll figure it out. just
miss you. follow the sun's trail, you always do.

the state of things.

at the beginning of the global pandemic, let's not
call it a pandie, and while it is overused
unprecedented times is annoying, but at least
gives respect to what this is, i was already
feeling this sludge in my heels. things were
already sticking to my calloused feet and
wearing me heavy. i had high-paying
employment that was well, high-paying and safe
by pandemic standards (pandie stands), cush by
others. but a heavy nagging feeling inside that
little pit in my stomach. a poke in my side when
i bent down to grovel when i made a mistake,
leaving my shirt gape open for stares, my behind
high and proud for approval. the man (white, of
course) who i reported to had been accused of
sexual misconduct is how i put it to my hopeful
future employers, really he was accused of rape.
which i knew when i accepted the job, laughed
at his jokes, sat in his apartment, refilled his
viagra and other sundry items that eventually
whittled me down to this stick figure here. but
the money! the money that i never took a
vacation with, the money that increased my
student loan payments that didnt make a dent in

the overall loan amount which is higher now
than it was when i was making $800 a month
payments, the money that did help me produce a
play that he came to see that overall cost about
$700 to put up. the money that didn't remind me
to bring my 11 year old dog in from the rain for
8 hours because i had to drive downtown for a
surprise audit. the money which i would now
fucking kill to have. but i quit that job because i
had a sneaking suspicion also known as a
conscious also known as morals also known as
jesus fucking christ what are you doing how can
you call yourself a feminist, a mentor an artist
you fucking opportunist that if i didn't leave i
wasnt being true to myself. so i left that very
secure, very high-paying job in April of 2020
which now seems like, well, a huge fucking
mistake. and i have to admit, when you think
things can't get any worse, they often do. get
worse that is, much worse. the world has no
standard for good or bad. things just happen and
we place that label on them and to even fuck it
all more, our individual labels are different. so,
yes every storm eventually runs out of rain, and
yes, things have to get better because of
whatever optimistic bullshit quote or verse or
poem you want to throw at me so that i can lift
my chin a little higher, and that's fine, i'll lift it
but only so you stop nagging me about it

because i know i'm only lifting it so that the
next southpaw hook has a clean target. at least i
have morals, though, right?

it will always be about you

"the moment you asked my name, i knew i'd be crying about you for the rest of my life" sounds like a country song, but is legit what i thought when you extended your hand. and so far, has proven mostly true. the only difference now i know and now i've resigned to these feelings about you and this dream about us and this disappointment in me. and this, this drivel, it's not about you, but it's also not not about you. it will always be about you.

just hold on

I swear though, it's not all about you. Or us being some definable thing that was easily categorized as an item, we've been talking for two years now how that don't make sense for us. And it never has. Two years before that I knew I loved you and we had never spoke, never shared anything beyond looks in between movements that felt like a kick in the stomach so yeah this shit is weird. There is some thread some surge some energy that exists between our hearts and it's the same piece of yarn that exists between you and your scattered thoughts that keep your body twitching at night and it's wrapped around the jumble of puzzle pieces I can't make fit in my 9-5 501c3 life. And when I dream which is rare so when I dream I know it's gotta mean something and I know I know I know I said I don't believe in that shit and I know I've been saying that I'm gonna stop making a sign out of every sign I see and that not all deals have to be a big deal but this one is. This dream I see from an aerial view I see a space that is full of art and I see a door that doesn't stay closed for long and I see hearts of energy coming and going and scraps and starts and overflowing words and

time to play and baskets to be shared full of
silliness and hope and a totally dope coffee and
tea spread and the air fryer gets used too much
but who cares? Because we have a home that is
for us and whoever or whatever wants to drop in
and create and stay or come back and I swear it's
not about you it's about this dream. It's about
what we dreamed of in the dark. It's what we
dreamed of when we were on the verge of giving
up and we tried one final time to pull ourselves
out of the darkness and the first source of light
we find was each other. And fuck the darkness is
so strong, stronger than we anticipated and it
dragged us down, it will always try to drag us
down. But my hand is still clutching onto your
knotted ties and I can't see the light in me but I
know it's there, I know because I see yours and
mine must be there too. And if we create a place
for our light to shine we can be a beacon. I'm
here. I'm ready to start building this, I don't
know what but I feel it needing to be built and at
a time when all my brain tells me is to give up
and resign to that life that is so formulaic and
been done and obvious and easy my heart holds
on. Hold on with me.

what i am

this is my body. it's female in nature, soft and padded in places you'd think, like where I sit, but not padded in places i used to dream about like my chest. i used to dream of the day i'd have breasts, cup my hands there and imagine filling out a Victoria's Secret padded bra. It never happened, but damn can i sport a deep v. and my legs are strong but not lean. i knew that when i was a sophomore in college walking across the quad and a classmate shouted "damn, molly's got big hips" which i think most women know what that shrinking feels like, before that i remember watching Tinkerbell measuring her hips and holding it up to her face appalled, I practiced that when I was 10 and perfected it at 15. Before that, I never learned to swim because I never learned to like my body. I have this very flat stomach that, sure you could say is contributed by my decision to never bear children and my flirting with a dangerous commitment to diet and exercise, but I do wonder what 4 years of constant brace wearing that was shaped like a corset did to my body while it was going through puberty. If women bind their feet… and I bound my body, not sure, but it has always been flat and my hip bones have always stuck out in the same way no matter my weight. I have large feet by other women's standards. And someone once told me that I have pretty hands. I used to like my neck and clavicles, but I don't know, they're kinda boney now. My shoulders are nice. And my hair is going gray, which is weird after a lifetime of dark brown hairs on my clothes and in my hairbrush to find white hairs in the drain and on my pillow make it seem like someone else's presence has left a calling card, but it's just me. I used to have a big smile that made my eyes squint, it got a lot of compliments at one time. It doesn't come out as often to play. I have lots of tattoos, bright colors of things that do and don't matter to me. I like those. I hope to add more soon. My body clicks and pops loudly, in my feet and ankles, my shoulders, and recently my right hip's gotta spot that demands to be popped daily. I have calluses. And scars. I'm not very flexible, but I try. I can run a mile in 8 minutes. I can do that with a broken heart.

forcing a poem (for you)

Hands tied to the pen, just cut me open it'll be faster. I'll bleed out on the page and you can derive the meaning from there. Hold it up to the light, read it upside down, bury it in the yard and see what comes up at the next full moon.

one final hope

all this? just silly, passing thoughts i have. no matter, no mind needed to pay for this matter. just a blip, a trip, a stumbling phrase, a wish, a desire. i'll recover, i'll reorder these bones. find some fresh ones on amazon or target dot com or some other reputable internet site that sells diluted home goods and shirts with capitalized phrasing. i'll sort through this clutter, probably leave most of it on the curb for free or refuse, trash i mean. can probably do without most of these, this dream about a home to create in, and this belief about how love can be, which is so saccharine and obviously out of reach for these small hands who have managed to hurt the most precious hearts i've encountered, yes those will go directly into the trash, not left for some innocent pure passerby to accidentally pick up and try to apply to their present, their future. best not spread those around. i'll toss out this want for a life with a higher purpose, it's remarkable how unremarkable our lives are, so yes, no need for that, held onto it longer than intended. i can let go of wanting to be seen, wanting this foolish line around independent partnership, that's a made-up phrase and those words don't even

make sense together, it was imagined some love
drunk or sun high day, just a little foolish thing,
time to let that go, impossible to dance it alone
anyway. and now, all this space for new shelving
and knickknacks, orderly stacks, matching paint,
monochromed and sharp. i really don't want to
get lost in the walls of my brain again, so i'll just
remove all soft things and cozy bits, not a place
for things to grow, no light to be let in, it's
unwelcoming sure, but that's my insides for ya.
it's time to move on, see what's grown up,
grown out of this. keeping it simple from now
on, no more foolery or hope. just serious
thoughts and attainable reaching, just tangible
gains less dancing, less dreaming. no more
clowning, no more your fool, no more artists
way or saging the house with windows open, no
more stargazing, no more wildflower fields, time
to cover up these bright tattoos, delete these
words. find my inner child and tell her that yes,
even she must grow up, get a job that doesn't
pay well but pays something. everyone's gotta
pull their weight around here, gotta pitch in with
something that is actually useful, dreams don't
pay the bills little girl. let's level up, yes, let go
of this silliness, a final hope - let it let go of me.